The Year of the Cookie

Delicious Recipes & Reasons to Eat Cookies Year-Round

Rose Dunnington

LARK BOOKS

A Division of Sterling Publishing Co., Inc.
New York / London

Library of Congress Cataloging-in-Publication Data

Dunnington, Rose.
The year of the cookie : delicious recipes & reasons to eat cookies year-round / Rose Dunnington. -- 1st ed.
  p. cm.
Includes index.
ISBN-13: 978-1-60059-237-9 (HC-PLC with concealed spiral : alk. paper)
ISBN-10: 1-60059-237-6 (HC-PLC with concealed spiral : alk. paper)
1. Cookies. 2. Holiday cookery. I. Title.
TX772.D867 2008
641.8'654--dc22

2008001053

10 9 8 7 6 5 4 3 2 1

First Edition

Published by Lark Books, A Division of Sterling Publishing Co., Inc.
387 Park Avenue South, New York, NY 10016

Text © 2008, Rose Dunnington
Photography © 2008, Lark Books

Distributed in Canada by Sterling Publishing,
c/o Canadian Manda Group, 165 Dufferin Street
Toronto, Ontario, Canada M6K 3H6

Distributed in the United Kingdom by GMC Distribution Services,
Castle Place, 166 High Street, Lewes, East Sussex, England BN7 1XU

Distributed in Australia by Capricorn Link (Australia) Pty Ltd.,
P.O. Box 704, Windsor, NSW 2756 Australia

If you have questions or comments about this book, please contact:
Lark Books
67 Broadway
Asheville, NC 28801
828-253-0467

Manufactured in China

ISBN 13: 978-1-60059-237-9

For information about custom editions, special sales, premium and corporate purchases, please contact Sterling Special Sales Department at 800-805-5489 or specialsales@sterlingpub.com.

Editor: Veronika Alice Gunter

Art Director: Robin Gregory

Cover Design: Celia Naranjo

Stylist: Skip Wade

Photographer: John Widman

Acknowledgments

A million thanks to models Willem, Kahlani, Jen, Henry, and Chloe. You're all lots of fun and marvelously good-looking.

Thank you, Veronika, for pulling it off yet again.

Thanks to Robin, Celia, Skip, John, and Stephen for making the book so beautiful.

Love and kisses to Steve for taste testing and dishwashing.

For my wonderful stepmother, Beverly Rosser Reitzel,
who is a big fan of cookies and parties.

Calendar of Cookies

The Recipes

Make Every Year the Year of the Cookie

Want to celebrate your favorite holidays with cookies? Need an excuse to make cookies any day? I've got you covered. This book is all about cookies: sweet, chewy, crispy, nutty, chocolaty, scrumptious cookies. A whole year's worth!

I've got **Gingerbread People** for Christmas, **Peek-a-boo Jelly Valentines** for (duh) St. Valentine's Day, and a **Giant Cookie** that's just right for your birthday. That should be a holiday—right? There are also cookies for celebrations that aren't traditionally about food, such as my **O'atmeal Raisin** for St. Patrick's Day, **Spring Spritz Flowers** for the spring equinox, and **Frosted Maple Leaves** for Canada Day.

I investigated holidays from around the world to find more cookie-making occasions. Never heard of the Lithuanian Day of the Serpents? That won't stop you from celebrating it with my yummy **Honey Wafers**. Same with the Indian Festival of Lights—you deserve delicious **Cashew Cardamom Coconut Cookies** no matter what continent you come from.

Not enough? I didn't think so. You'd be amazed by how many holidays are out there. All beg to be commemorated with a special cookie, of course. Make **Arrr-some Molassies** for Talk Like a Pirate Day, and **Stealthy Chocolate Cookies** for Day of the Ninja. Dunk **Chocolate Almond Biscotti** into a cuppa joe on Joe Day. (That's when everyone who hates his name is called Joe.)

This book is totally easy to use, whether you're just learning to cook or you're already a whiz in the kitchen. It starts with a basics section with loads of pictures. I'll walk you through every step of cookie making, from reading a recipe to storing your tasty creations. Even if you've made hundreds of batches of cookies, I bet you'll learn something new. The glossaries at the back of the book are handy when you want to remind yourself what a cooking term means, or what a tool looks like.

Are you ready to get started? Come on! Make this the Year of the Cookie!

Cookie Basics

Have you picked out your first recipe to try? If I don't have a cookie for today's date, remember that Wednesday always deserves a celebration. So does Thursday, for that matter. And Friday, and. . .well, you know what I mean. Let's get started!

First Things First

Read the recipe all the way through. Make sure you have everything you need and enough time to finish. The **yield** tells you how much each recipe makes. If you're unfamiliar with a piece of equipment or a term, check back in this section or look in the glossaries (pages 108-110).

Take off any rings, bracelets, and watches that you don't want gunked up with cookie dough. Wash your hands, tie back your hair if it's long, and put on an apron. No apron? Ask your dad for an old shirt you can wear. Bribe him with cookies if you need to.

Measuring

Master the ancient art of measuring to get just the cookie you want. Use **liquid measuring cups** for liquids, such as milk, and **solid measuring cups** for solids, such as flour. **Measuring spoons** work for liquids and solids.

Liquid measuring cups usually have tons of lines, numbers, and abbreviations, such as ml and oz. Figure out which line marks the measurement you want, and pour up to that line. The best way to get an accurate measurement is to put the cup on a stable surface and put your eyes even with the top of the liquid.

Dry **ingredients** are measured in scoop-type measuring cups. Scoop the ingredient up in the cup. Use the flat edge of a table knife against the rim of the cup to push the extra off the top. Also use this method to measure tablespoons and teaspoons of dry ingredients.

It may seem like the amounts of baking soda and baking powder are too tiny to do anything. Don't be fooled! These are powerful ingredients. Too much tastes gross. (You can slop around some with the other ingredients, and you'll still have delicious cookies.)

Sometimes a recipe calls for brown sugar or coconut to be **packed**. This means you jam it down in the measuring cup, packing it full. Don't pack other ingredients.

Butter, Zest & Nuts

A few ingredients need to be prepared before you use them. Most of my recipes call for using **softened** butter, which is a bit mushy. Soften butter by leaving it on a kitchen counter for a few hours or microwave it for 5 or 10 seconds. (Unwrap the butter and cut it into chunks before microwaving it, or the center of the stick will melt while the rest is still cold.)

A

A recipe may call for a citrus fruit's **zest**. To create zest, first rinse the fruit under hot water, and then rub it against a **microplane grater** or the small holes of a **box grater**. (See photo A.) Press the fruit down and away from you. Use only the colored part of the rind for zest.

Some of my recipes use nuts—pecans, walnuts, almonds, etc. If you have a food allergy or are making cookies for someone who does, you can leave them out. Sometimes I use a **food processor** to grind nuts, instead of using a small knife to cut them into tiny pieces. Follow the manufacturer's instructions for your food processor. Unplug it before you reach inside.

Mixing

I use an **electric mixer** to combine ingredients. Make sure to unplug your mixer before you change attachments or lick the **beaters**. I didn't have an electric mixer when I was a kid. (That's code for "I broke the mixer." Or maybe my brother or sister did.) Anyway, the point is that I know for sure you can also mix dough with a fork and your muscles. It just takes longer. Here are some mixing terms you'll see often in this book:

Cream

To **cream** is to mix softened butter and sugar with the mixer on medium-high speed. Thorough creaming incorporates plenty of air into the mixture and dissolves the sugar. To do this, first put the sugar and butter in a mixing bowl. (See photo B.) Then mix. (See photo C.) The mixture should look light and fluffy. If you rub a bit between your fingers, you should only feel a few sugar granules, or none at all. Achieving the right

B

C

consistency means your cookies spread less in the oven. (This is a good thing.)

Beat

You **beat** eggs and other ingredients to mix them into a dough. Usually you set the mixer on medium speed. First, crack the eggshell on the edge of the bowl. Then drop the egg white and yolk together into the bowl. Discard the shell. Beat! The mixture will look clumpy and gross at this stage. (See photo D.) No problem! That's just how it is.

Whites or Yolks?

Sometimes you just want to use the white or yolk of an egg. Here's how: Crack the egg over a bowl, and then open it so the two halves are little cups. Gently pass the egg from one half of the shell to the other. Let the egg white ooze out, and keep the yolk. After a few passes, you'll have all the white in the bowl, and the yolk in the shell. (See photo.) This is called separating an egg. Wash your hands after touching raw eggs.

D

If the butter stays stuck to the sides of the bowl, it won't mix with the eggs. Scrape the bowl down with a rubber spatula if you see that happening. Then beat the mixture a bit more, to evenly mix everything.

Mix or Knead

When a recipe tells you to mix, set the mixer on a low speed and blend everything just until it's evenly combined. Don't overdo it—unless you like tough cookies.

Finish mixing stiff dough by **kneading**. Dump the dough on a floured pastry board and mash it with the heels of your hands. Turn the dough, and mash it again until all the crumbs stick together.

Whip or Fold

Whipping adds air to food. It's an important step for the meringue used in the Ghostly

E

Kisses (Happy Halloween!) on page 84. Set the mixer on high speed until the mixture forms soft peaks. (See photo E.)

Folding is a gentle way to add ingredients without changing the consistency of the dough. With a rubber spatula, incorporate the ingredients using a sideways stirring motion.

Shaping Cookies

Some cookies get special treatment to make them extra fancy or cool looking. The rest are **drop cookies**, like Hunkka Love Chunks (to celebrate Elvis' birthday) on page 20. For drop cookies, just glop spoonfuls of the dough onto the **cookie sheet**. Be sure to leave plenty of room between cookies. (They spread as they bake.)

Some doughs need to be **chilled** before shaping, such as Apricot Hamantashen (see page 44). That makes the dough easier to work with. To chill, wrap dough in plastic wrap. Then mash it into a disc shape and put that in the fridge. Each recipe will tell you the specifics about how to prepare its dough, but at a minimum you must chill dough for 15 minutes.

If your dough gets too soft or sticky to work with, rewrap it and chill it again.

Rolling Dough

Rolling out dough is easy. You do the work on a lightly floured **pastry board**. **Flour** the **rolling pin**, lay it on the dough, and push away from you for a few gentle rolls. Give the dough a quarter turn. Do a few more rolls. Turn and roll the dough until it's the thickness called for in the recipe. (See photo F.) You're done!

F

Using Cookie Cutters

Want to cut your dough into fun shapes? Grab a **cookie cutter**. Dip its sharp edge in flour so it won't stick to the dough. Then push it straight down through the dough. (NO twisting.) **Cutout cookies** don't spread as much as drop cookies, but you still need to leave some space between them as they bake.

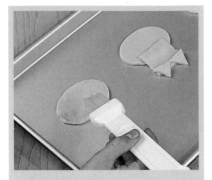

Eggwash

Some cookies have unusual shapes that you create by connecting pieces of dough. To make cookies like these, cut out the shapes called for in the instructions. Then mix up some eggwash: crack an egg into a small bowl, add about a tablespoon of water, and mix with a fork. Start assembling your cookies on a greased cookie sheet. Use a pastry brush or your fingers to paint on a little eggwash where the pieces overlap. (See photo.) Press down lightly on the seams where the pieces touch to join them. Wash your hands well before sliding the cookies into the oven for baking.

Baking

Preheating gets the oven to just the right temperature to **bake**. There are a few ways to keep your cookies from sticking to the cookie sheet. Using a so-called "non-stick" cookie sheet is not one of them. (Those things never work!) **Greasing** the pan is easy—you just smear a little oil or butter on the sheet. I like to use the inside of the butter wrapper. (See photo G.) Cooking spray works, but you have to hold your breath!

G

Parchment paper keeps cookies from sticking, but I think it's a wasteful solution. For some cookies, though, such as Benne Wafers (to celebrate Kwanzaa) on page 104, parchment paper works best. Remember that you can use the same sheet several times—flip it when one side gets crumbly. And don't mix up waxed paper with parchment paper. Wax-flavored cookies taste terrible.

To bake cookie dough, you'll place the loaded cookie sheet as close to the center of the oven as you can. That's because heat comes from the bottom of the oven, and heat rises, so the food gets cooked from all directions.

Unless your dad is a caterer or your mom is a chef, you probably won't have enough cookie sheets to bake all your cookies in one **batch**. No problem! Just bake the first batch, let the cookies cool a bit, and then move them to a wire cooling rack. Now your sheet is free for more cookie dough. Watch out—it's still hot. Most cookie dough will do just fine on a warm cookie sheet. For a few recipes, the sheet needs to be cool. Just run cold water over the cookie sheet and dry it before you bake the next batch.

Decorating

About half of the cookies in this book are made with **icing** (also called **frosting**). Icing is a fun way to add color and character to a cookie. Just look at the Day of the Dead Zany Skulls on page 88. Imagine how lifeless they'd be without icing! Icing also tastes great. Here are the basics for making icing and using it to decorate your cookies. Recipes for several kinds of **glazes** are included with their cookies.

Royal Icing

Recipes for cookies that need stiff icing will refer you to this recipe. It's super easy to make.

What You Need
- 1 egg
- 1¼ cup confectioners' sugar
- mixing bowl
- mixer or whisk

1 Separate the egg and drop the egg white into the mixing bowl. (See page 12.) Add the sugar to the egg.

2 Mix using the lowest speed. Once the ingredients begin to combine, whip at the highest speed until the icing is snow-white and fluffy.

Buttercream Frosting

For thick, delicious icing, this is this recipe. Don't eat it all before decorating your cookies! (Or just make another batch.)

What You Need
- 1 stick (½ cup) softened butter
- 4 cups powdered sugar
- 2 teaspoons vanilla extract
- 3 to 4 tablespoons milk
- mixing bowl
- mixer

1 Put all the ingredients in a mixing bowl, and mix using medium to high speeds until you have a smooth, creamy mixture.

Making and Using a Pastry Bag

Use a pastry bag to draw with icing. You can buy one or just make one. I make one bag for each color of icing I need.

What You Need
- waxed paper or parchment paper
- flat surface
- scissors
- spatula or spoon
- icing or frosting

1 Lay one sheet of waxed paper flat on your work surface. Fold up one bottom corner to create a triangle. Cut along the fold. (See photo A.)

A

B

C

2 Roll one point from the base (long side) of the triangle toward the top point of the triangle. (See photo B.)

3 Bring the other base point around to form a cone. (See photo C.)

continued on next page

4 Shuffle the paper so that the inside piece is tightening while the outer piece continues to wrap into a cone. (See photo D.)

5 Fold in the pieces at the top of the cone to hold the shape in place. (See photo E.)

6 Use a spatula or spoon to fill the bag half full with icing. Shake the icing down into the tip to avoid air pockets.

7 Fold up the end of the bag to seal it. Cut the tip to make a small hole. (See photo F.)

8 Practice piping on a sheet of waxed paper. (See photo G.) You'll hold the pointy end of the pastry bag with one hand to guide it and use your other hand to squeeze the end of the bag. Continue folding the bag as it empties.

9 When you are finished practicing, use the same technique on a cookie. Throw the pastry bag away after you use and/or eat all of the icing out of it.

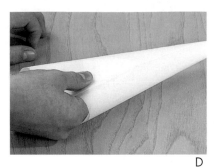

D

E

F

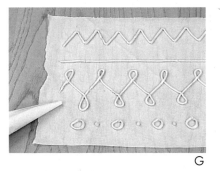

G

Cooling, Storing, Clean Up

When cookies first come out of the oven, they tend to be too soft to hold their shape. Let them sit on the pan for a couple minutes to firm up. Then use a **metal spatula** to move them to a **wire cooling rack**. The rack lets air circulate all around each cookie, so it cools without getting soggy. Store your cookies in a sealed container at room temperature for several days. Several days? Who am I kidding? Eat 'em!

All that's left to do is to clean up after yourself. Don't forget! Show your family how easy it is to make cookies AND keep the kitchen clean. Then they'll be psyched to know that you'll be making cookies year-round!

The
Recipes

equipment

- measuring cups and spoons
- mixing bowl
- electric mixer
- rubber spatula
- lightly floured pastry board
- plastic wrap
- paring knife
- cookie sheet, lined with parchment paper
- oven mitts

Yield: about 50 coins—plenty for lots and lots of luck

ingredients

- 2 sticks (1 cup) butter, softened
- ½ cup sugar
- zest of 1 big lemon, or 2 little lemons
- ⅛ teaspoon salt
- 2 cups flour, sifted
- yellow sparkle sugar

New Year's Day
January 1

Lucky Lemony Coins

A tradition says that the more black-eyed peas you eat on New Year's Day, the more money you'll have that year. Come on—black-eyed peas? Gimme cookies!

1 Cream the softened butter with the sugar, zest, and salt. Use the rubber spatula to scrape down the beaters and the sides of the bowl.

2 Dump the flour into the bowl with the butter mixture. Use your fingertips to rub the flour into the butter. (The hand motion is like the gesture that means "money." Do you recognize a theme here?)

3 Squish the crumbly dough together until it forms a ball. Dump the ball of dough onto the board, and knead it several times. Divide the dough in half, and shape each half into a ball. Put the balls back in the mixing bowl.

4 Wipe any stray clumps of dough off of the pastry board. Sprinkle a few tablespoons of yellow sparkle sugar on the board. Roll one of the dough balls into a long, sugarcoated snake, about 1 inch in diameter. Wrap the snake in plastic. Do the same thing with the other half of dough. Freeze the snakes for half an hour.

5 Preheat the oven to 350°F. Unwrap one of the chilled dough snakes and put it on the board. Cut the dough into ¼-inch thick slices. Put them on the cookie sheet ½ inch apart. Repeat with the rest of the dough.

6 Bake the cookies 8 to 10 minutes, until they look dry on top, but are still pale. Use oven mitts to take the cookie sheet out of the oven. These little cookies are very delicate, so don't try to move them until they cool. Good luck this year!

Elvis Presley's Birthday
January 8

Hunkka Love Chunks

Curl your lip and shake your hips! It's all about attitude when you celebrate the King of Rock and Roll's birthday. Elvis would love this peanut butter and chocolate cookie.

equipment

- measuring cups and spoons
- mixing bowl
- electric mixer
- wooden spoon
- greased cookie sheet
- spoon
- fork
- oven mitts
- metal spatula
- wire cooling rack

Yield: about 4 dozen cookies

ingredients

- 2 sticks (1 cup) butter, softened
- 1 cup sugar
- 1 cup (packed) brown sugar
- 2 eggs
- 2 teaspoons vanilla extract
- 2 cups peanut butter
- 2½ cups flour
- 1 teaspoon baking soda
- ½ teaspoon salt
- Two 4-ounce bars semisweet chocolate

1 Preheat the oven to 375°F. Cream the butter, sugar, and brown sugar. Add the eggs, vanilla extract, and peanut butter. Beat until well blended.

2 Add the flour, baking soda, and salt to the peanut butter mixture. Mix until you don't see any streaks of flour.

3 While they're still in their wrappers, break the chocolate bars into raisin-sized chunks. Unwrap the chunks and use the wooden spoon to stir them into the cookie dough.

4 Roll spoonfuls of dough into balls with your hands. Place the balls a few inches apart on the cookie sheet. Use the fork to mash them flat, first one way, then perpendicularly, to make a grid design.

5 Bake for 8 to 10 minutes. Use oven mitts to take the cookies out of the oven. Use the metal spatula to move the hot cookies to the cooling rack. Practice your Elvis impersonation while you wait for them to cool.

equipment

- measuring cups and spoons
- mixing bowl
- electric mixer
- wooden spoon
- greased cookie sheet
- spoon
- oven mitts
- metal spatula
- wire cooling rack

Yield: about 4 dozen cookies

ingredients

- 2 sticks (1 cup) butter, softened
- 2/3 cup sugar
- 2/3 cup (packed) brown sugar
- 2 eggs
- 2 teaspoons vanilla extract
- 2 1/2 cups flour
- 1 teaspoon baking soda
- 1/2 teaspoon salt
- 2/3 cup chocolate chips
- 2/3 cup white chocolate chips
- 2/3 cup butterscotch chips

Martin Luther King, Jr. Day
mid-January

Sweet Dreams

Dr. Martin Luther King Jr. was one of the all-time best human beings. Celebrate his dream and yours with cookies that combine delicious flavors.

1 Preheat the oven to 375°F. Cream the butter, sugar, and brown sugar. Add the eggs and vanilla extract. Beat until well blended.

2 Add the flour, baking soda, and salt to the butter mixture, and mix until you don't see any streaks of flour.

3 Stir all the chips into the cookie dough with the wooden spoon.

4 Drop spoonfuls of dough a couple inches apart on the cookie sheet. Bake the cookies for 8 to 10 minutes.

5 Use oven mitts to take the hot cookies out of the oven. Use the metal spatula to move them to the cooling rack. When you bite into these dreamy cookies, think about how much better America is, thanks to Dr. King and the civil rights workers.

Good Fortune Cookies

Write your own predictions and bake them into these fun, tasty, folded cookies.

Yield: 12 cookies

ingredients

- ½ cup sliced almonds
- ½ cup sugar
- ¼ teaspoon salt
- ½ cup flour
- 2 egg whites
- ¼ cup cooking oil
- ½ teaspoon vanilla extract
- ½ teaspoon almond extract

equipment

- pen
- 12 strips of paper 4 inches long and ½ inch wide
- measuring cups and spoons
- food processor
- fork
- mixing bowl
- spoon
- cookie sheet, lined with parchment paper
- small offset spatula
- oven mitts
- thin cotton gloves, or two pairs of latex gloves
- metal spatula
- coffee mug
- muffin tin

1 Preheat the oven to 350°F. Write funny fortunes on the strips of paper. Grind the almonds and sugar in the food processor until the mixture is sandy. Add the salt and flour, and pulse to combine.

2 Use the fork to lightly beat the egg whites, oil, vanilla extract, and almond extract together in the mixing bowl. Add the almond mixture and mix.

3 Spoon a heaping tablespoon of batter on a parchment paper-lined cookie sheet. Use the small offset spatula to spread the batter into a circle about 4 inches across. The batter should be super-thin—you'll see patches of the paper through it. Bake the cookie 7 to 8 minutes, until the edges begin to brown. Use oven mitts to take the pan out of the oven.

4 Wear the gloves to form the hot cookie. You'll have to work fast. Use the metal spatula to flip a cookie into your hand. Lay a fortune on it. Fold the cookie in half over the fortune, and pinch it closed. Gently pull the corners down over the lip of the coffee mug. (See photo above.) Put the finished cookie in a muffin tin to hold its shape as it cools.

5 Repeat steps 3 and 4 with the rest of the batter. If your cookies split when you fold them, you need to spread the batter thinner. Always let the cookie sheets cool before you put more batter on them. Once you get the hang of shaping the cookies, bake 2 or 3 at a time.

equipment

- measuring cups and spoons
- mixing bowl
- electric mixer
- plastic wrap
- lightly floured pastry board
- rolling pin
- flower-shaped cookie cutter
- greased cookie sheet
- oven mitts
- metal spatula
- wire cooling rack

Yield: 3 to 4 dozen cookies, depending on the size of your cookie cutter

ingredients

- 1 stick (1/2 cup) butter, softened
- 1/2 cup sugar
- 1/2 cup honey
- 2 cups flour
- 1/2 teaspoon salt
- 1/4 teaspoon baking soda
- 1/2 teaspoon ground cinnamon
- 1/2 teaspoon lemon zest
- sliced almonds

Kirmeline—Day of the Serpents
January 25

Honey Wafers

This Lithuanian holiday celebrates the waking of hibernating animals. (That means spring is nearing!) Enjoy the cookies, but avoid snakes and bees.

1 Cream the butter and sugar. Add the honey. Beat until the concoction stiffens back up to the texture it was before you added the honey.

2 Mix the flour, salt, baking soda, cinnamon, and lemon zest into the butter mixture. Blend the ingredients well. Divide the dough in half. Wrap each half in plastic wrap, and mash them into discs about 1/2 inch thick. Chill the cookie dough for at least 30 minutes.

3 Preheat the oven to 375°F. Sprinkle flour on the rolling pin. Working with one disc of chilled dough at a time, roll the dough out to about 1/4 inch thick. Use the cookie cutter to cut out flower shapes. Squish the dough scraps together. Repeat all the wrapping, mashing, chilling, rolling, and cutting with the scraps.

4 Place the flowers 1 inch apart on the cookie sheet. Gently press sliced almonds on the cookies. Bake 8 to 10 minutes.

5 Use oven mitts to remove the cookies from the oven. Let them cool on the pan for a couple of minutes. Use the spatula to transfer the warm cookies to the cooling rack.

Sticky-Sweet Twigs & Berries

These cookies will put you in such a good mood, you'll be happy with whatever the groundhog predicts. Don't feed these treats to any wildlife—they're for you!

Yield: 3 to 4 dozen cookies, depending on how big you make them

ingredients

- ½ stick (¼ cup) butter
- 10.5-ounce bag of mini marshmallows
- ¼ cup peanut butter
- 1 cup dried cranberries
- Two 5-ounce cans chow mein noodles

1 Melt the butter, marshmallows, and peanut butter over medium-low heat. Use the wooden spoon to stir the mixture until it's all the same color.

2 While the goopy mixture is melting, use your fingers to break apart any clumps of cranberries. Add the chow mein noodles and cranberries to the melted goop. Stir until well coated.

3 Glop spoonfuls of the mixture onto the greased waxed paper. It helps to use the rubber spatula to push it off the spoon. Don't be tempted to push it off with your finger—this stuff is hotter than it looks.

4 Let the cookies cool for at least 20 minutes. Meanwhile, try to figure out the connections between groundhogs, shadows, and snow. It's a mystery to me..

equipment

- measuring cups and spoons
- mixing bowl
- electric mixer
- plastic wrap
- lightly floured pastry board
- rolling pin
- large heart-shaped cookie cutter
- small heart-shaped cookie cutter
- greased cookie sheet
- pastry brush
- spoon
- oven mitts
- metal spatula
- wire cooling rack

Yield: about 3 dozen valentines

ingredients

- 2 sticks (1 cup) butter, softened
- 1½ cups sugar
- 2 eggs
- 1 tablespoon vanilla extract
- 3 cups flour
- ½ teaspoon salt
- egg wash (page 14)
- raspberry jam

St. Valentine's Day
February 14

Peek-a-boo Jelly Valentines

Share these with people you love. Or someone you like. Or someone you **like** like—I won't tell.

1 Cream the butter and sugar. Add the eggs and vanilla extract. Beat until well blended.

2 Mix the flour and salt into the butter mixture. Half the dough. Wrap each half in plastic wrap, and mash them into discs about ½ inch thick. Chill the cookie dough for at least 15 minutes.

3 Preheat the oven to 375°F. Sprinkle flour on the rolling pin. Working with one disc of chilled dough at a time, roll the dough out to about ¼ inch thick. Cut large hearts out of the dough. Cut small hearts out of half of the large hearts, to create outlines.

4 Squish the dough scraps, including the small hearts, together. Repeat all the wrapping, mashing, chilling, rolling, and cutting. Remember to make equal numbers of large hearts and outlines.

5 Place the large hearts 1 inch apart on the cookie sheet. Brush egg wash on the perimeter of the cookies, where the outlines will go. Spread jam on the middle area. Top each jammy heart with a dough outline.

6 Bake these cookies for 10 to 12 minutes. Use oven mitts to remove the cookies from the oven. Then use the metal spatula to move the hot cookies to the cooling rack. When the valentines are cool, spread the love!

Pecan Tassies

New Orleans hosts America's largest Mardi Gras party. So why not celebrate the holiday with a big, easy cookie? Mini pecan pies, anyone?

equipment

- measuring cups and spoons
- mixing bowl
- electric mixer
- lightly floured pastry board
- plastic wrap
- ungreased muffin tin (Paper liners are optional.)
- fork
- spoon
- oven mitts
- table knife
- wire cooling rack
- sifter

Yield: 1 dozen tassies

ingredients

- 4 ounces (half of an 8-ounce package) of cream cheese, softened
- 1 stick (½ cup) butter, softened
- 1 cup flour
- 1 egg
- ¾ cup (packed) light brown sugar
- 1 teaspoon vanilla extract
- 1 cup pecan pieces
- powdered sugar

1 Cream the cream cheese and butter. Add the flour, and mix until the dough comes together in a ball. Dump the dough out onto the board, and knead the dough several times. Wrap the dough in plastic wrap. Chill the dough for about an hour.

2 Preheat the oven to 350°F. Roll the chilled dough into 2-inch balls. Pop the balls into the muffin tins. Press the dough into the tins to make little cups. Each dough cup will only reach about halfway up the muffin cup.

3 Crack the egg into a liquid measuring cup. Use the fork to beat the egg, brown sugar, and vanilla extract until evenly blended. Divide the pecans among the dough cups. Pour in enough of the egg mixture to cover the pecans. (I use a spoon to catch drips from the measuring cup's spout.)

4 Bake the tassies for 20 to 25 minutes. Use oven mitts to remove the tassies from the oven. Let them cool for 10 minutes, and then use the table knife to turn them out of the tins. Finish cooling on the wire rack. Sift powdered sugar over the cooled tassies.

equipment

- measuring cups and spoons
- mixing bowl
- electric mixer
- microplane grater
- plastic wrap
- lightly floured pastry board
- rolling pin
- number-shaped cookie cutters
- greased cookie sheet
- knife and cutting board
- strainer
- whisk
- oven mitts
- metal spatula
- wire cooling rack
- waxed paper
- spoon

ingredients

- 2 sticks (1 cup) butter, softened
- 1½ cups sugar
- 2 eggs
- 1 tablespoon vanilla extract
- 1 orange
- 3 cups flour
- ½ teaspoon salt
- 1 pound (4 cups) powdered sugar
- sprinkles

Pi Day
March 14

Orange Yum Numbers

What do you get when you divide a cookie's circumference by its diameter? Pi Day.

Yield: pi to thirty-six digits, which is this:
3.141592653589793238462643383327950288

1 Cream the butter and sugar. Add the eggs and vanilla extract. Beat until well blended. Zest the orange. You'll get about 1 tablespoon of zest. Add all of it to the bowl. Mix it in.

2 Mix the flour and the salt into the butter mixture. Divide the dough in half. Wrap each half in plastic wrap. Mash them into discs about ½ inch thick. Chill the dough for at least 30 minutes.

3 Preheat the oven to 375°F. Sprinkle flour on the rolling pin. Working with one disc of chilled dough at a time, roll the dough out to about ¼ inch thick. Use the cookie cutters to cut out each number of pi. Squish the dough scraps together. Repeat all the wrapping, mashing, chilling, rolling, and cutting.

4 Place the numbers 1 inch apart on the cookie sheet. Bake them for 8 to 10 minutes. Meanwhile, cut the orange in half and squeeze the juice into a strainer set over a liquid measuring cup. Subtract juice or add water to make ½ cup. Whisk the powdered sugar and juice together to make a glaze.

5 Use oven mitts to remove the cookies from the oven. Let the cookies cool a bit and then transfer them to the wire rack. Lay waxed paper under the rack. Spoon glaze over the warm cookies. Shake sprinkles onto the wet glaze.

O'atmeal Raisin

These scrumptious cookies are better than a pot of gold. Add a couple drops of green food coloring to your glass of milk for a festive St. Patty's Day look.

Yield: 3 to 4 dozen cookies, depending on how big you make them

ingredients

- 2 sticks (1 cup) butter, softened
- $2/3$ cup sugar
- $2/3$ cup (packed) brown sugar
- 2 eggs
- 2 teaspoons vanilla extract
- $1\frac{1}{2}$ cups flour
- 1 teaspoon baking soda
- $\frac{1}{2}$ teaspoon salt
- 1 teaspoon ground cinnamon
- $1\frac{1}{2}$ cup quick oats (not instant or old-fashioned)
- 1 cup walnut pieces (optional)
- $1\frac{1}{2}$ cups raisins

1 Preheat the oven to 375°F. Cream the butter, sugar, and brown sugar. Add the eggs and vanilla extract. Beat until the ingredients are well blended.

2 Add the flour, baking soda, salt, and cinnamon to the wet mixture. Mix until you don't see any streaks of flour.

3 Add the oats, walnuts, and raisins. Use the wooden spoon to stir the dough until all the goodies are evenly distributed.

4 Spoon the dough onto the cookie sheet, leaving a couple inches between each cookie. Bake for 8 to 10 minutes.

5 Use the oven mitts to remove the cookies from the oven. Use the metal spatula to move the hot cookies to the cooling rack. Dance an Irish jig to pass the time until the cookies are cool enough to eat.

equipment

- measuring cups and spoons
- mixing bowl
- electric mixer
- wooden spoon
- greased 12-inch pizza pan
- oven mitts
- pastry bag with star tip

Yield: one giant cookie, 8 to 10 servings

ingredients

- 1 stick ($1/2$ cup) butter, softened
- $1/3$ cup sugar
- $1/3$ cup (packed) brown sugar
- 1 egg
- 1 teaspoon vanilla extract
- $1 1/4$ cups flour
- $1/2$ teaspoon baking soda
- $1/4$ teaspoon salt
- 1 cup chocolate chips
- 1 cup chopped pecans
- Buttercream Frosting (page 15) or whipped cream

My Birthday
March 20

Giant Cookie

Happy birthday to me! Sure, you could make a giant cookie for someone else's special day. But let's not lose sight of what's really important: It's my birthday!

1 Preheat the oven to 375°F. Cream the butter, sugar, and brown sugar. Add the egg and vanilla extract. Beat until well blended.

2 Add the flour, baking soda, and salt to the wet mixture, and blend until you don't see any streaks of flour.

3 Stir the chocolate chips and pecans into the cookie dough with the wooden spoon. Dump the dough onto the pizza pan. Spread it in an even layer with the back of the spoon.

4 Bake the giant cookie 15 to 18 minutes. Use oven mitts to remove the cookie from the oven. Let the cookie cool before you decorate it with frosting and candles. When I blow out my candles, I wish for world peace and cookies for everyone. (See? I'm not totally selfish.)

Spring Spritz Flowers

Make a whole garden of these tasty little cookies to celebrate the first day of spring.

Yield: around 7 dozen flowers (You read it right—7 dozen.)

equipment

- measuring cups and spoons
- mixing bowl
- electric mixer
- cookie press and flower-shaped discs
- lightly greased cookie sheet
- oven mitts
- metal spatula
- wire cooling rack

ingredients

- 2 sticks (1 cup) butter, softened
- 3/4 cup sugar
- 2 egg yolks (page 12)
- 1 1/2 teaspoons almond or vanilla extract—your choice
- 2 1/2 cups flour
- 1/2 teaspoon baking powder
- 1/4 teaspoon salt
- food coloring
- decorations such as maraschino cherries, chocolate chips, and sprinkles

1 Preheat the oven to 375°F. Cream the butter and sugar. Add the egg yolks and flavoring. Beat until well combined. Add the flour, baking powder, and salt. Mix until the ingredients form dough.

2 Divide the dough into three to six parts. (It just depends on how many different shapes and colors you want to make.) Add a drop or so of food coloring to each part. Squish the dough until the color is evenly blended.

3 Follow the manufacturer's instructions to load your cookie press. Press out one cookie at a time, directly onto the cookie sheet. Don't worry if the first few cookies aren't perfect.

4 Click out cookies, about an inch apart, until the dough runs out or the cookie sheet is full. Press a decoration into each flower's center. Bake for 7 to 9 minutes, until you see the tiniest bit of tan on the bottom edge of a cookie.

5 Use oven mitts to remove the cookies from the oven. Let them cool for a couple of minutes, and then use the spatula to move the cookies to the wire rack to cool completely.

6 Reload the press with more dough, and a different flower-shaped disc. Let the cookie sheet cool before you press another batch of cookies on it, or the dough won't stick. Keep pressing and baking until you've used all of your dough.

equipment

- measuring cups and spoons
- mixing bowl
- electric mixer
- pastry board
- greased cookie sheet
- oven mitts
- metal spatula
- wire cooling rack
- serrated knife
- cutting board

Yield: about 20 biscotti

ingredients

- 2½ cups flour
- 1¼ cups sugar
- ¼ cup cocoa powder
- 1 teaspoon baking soda
- ⅛ teaspoon salt
- 3 eggs
- 1 teaspoon vanilla extract
- 2 teaspoons almond extract
- ⅔ cup mini chocolate chips
- 2 cups sliced almonds

Chocolate Almond Biscotti

Don't like your name? Call yourself Joe—that's what you do on this holiday. Then dunk these crunchy cookies in a cuppa joe (coffee!) or milk.

1 Preheat the oven to 350°F. Put the flour, sugar, cocoa powder, baking soda, and salt in the mixing bowl. Mix on low speed until well combined. Add the eggs, vanilla extract, and almond extract. Beat on medium until you have goopy dough. Mix in the chocolate chips.

2 Arrange ½ cup of the sliced almonds on the pastry board in a layer about 8 inches long and 5 inches wide. Glop half of the dough on top of the almonds. Scatter another ½ cup of almonds on top of the dough. Form the dough into a flattened, almond-covered loaf, and put it on the cookie sheet.

3 Repeat step 2 with the remaining dough, leaving a few inches between the loaves on the cookie sheet. Bake 40 minutes. Use oven mitts to remove the loaves from the oven. Let the loaves cool on the pan for a couple of minutes. Then use the metal spatula to transfer them to the cooling rack.

4 When the loaves are all the way cool, use the serrated knife to slice them diagonally into ½ inch thick biscotti. (If this is difficult, ask an adult to help.) Bake the biscotti for 5 to 7 minutes. Flip them over, and bake for another 5 to 7 minutes. Let them cool—then dunk!

Purim
March (sometimes in April)

Apricot Hamantashen

Purim is my friend Robert's favorite Jewish holiday because these are his favorite cookies.

Yield: about 2 dozen hamantashen

equipment

- measuring cups and spoons
- mixing bowl
- electric mixer
- plastic wrap
- lightly floured pastry board
- rolling pin
- 3-inch round cookie cutter
- greased cookie sheet
- spoon
- oven mitts
- metal spatula
- wire cooling rack

ingredients

- 1 stick (½ cup) butter, softened
- ½ cup sugar
- 1 egg
- 2 tablespoons orange juice
- 2 cups flour
- 1 teaspoon baking powder
- 1 tablespoon poppy seeds
- apricot preserves

1 Cream the butter and sugar. Add the egg and orange juice. Beat well. Add the flour, baking powder, and poppy seeds. Mix well.

2 Divide the dough in half. Wrap each half in plastic wrap. Mash the dough into flat discs. Chill for 2 hours, or overnight.

3 Preheat the oven to 375°F. Lightly flour the rolling pin. Working with one disc of dough at a time, roll the dough out to ¼ inch thick. Use the cookie cutter to cut out circles. Put them on the cookie sheet. Squish your dough scraps together. Chill them, roll them out, and cut out more cookies.

4 Spoon about 2 teaspoons of preserves onto the middle of each circle. Fold three sides of the circle over the filling, and pinch them together. (See photo.)

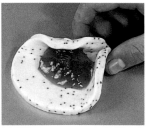

5 Bake the hamantashen for 10 to 12 minutes, until the corners are slightly browned. Use oven mitts to remove the cookies from the oven. Use the metal spatula to move the cookies to the wire rack to cool. Maybe these will be your favorite cookies, too!

equipment

- measuring cups and spoons
- box grater
- mixing bowl
- greased cookie sheet
- oven mitts
- metal spatula
- wire cooling rack
- rubber band

Yield: about 2 dozen savory cookies

ingredients

- ½ pound sharp white cheddar cheese
- ½ stick (¼ cup) butter, softened
- ½ cup flour
- ½ cup quick oats (not instant or old-fashioned)
- ¼ teaspoon salt
- ½ teaspoon hot sauce
- ¼ cup black olives, chopped into chocolate chunk-sized pieces
- ¼ cup chopped walnuts

April Fool's Day
April 1

Cheesy Tricks

Looks like a chewy chocolate chunk cookie, tastes like...olives and cheese! These savory treats are so tasty, your victims will ask to be fooled again.

1 Preheat the oven to 400°F. Grate the cheese. (Don't use pre-grated cheese; it usually contains an additive to keep the pieces separated.)

2 Put the cheese, butter, flour, oats, salt, and hot sauce into the bowl. Use your hands to mash the ingredients together until you have crumbly dough. Mix in the olives and walnuts.

3 Put cookie-sized gobs of dough 1 inch apart on the cookie sheet. These cheesy guys don't spread and puff as much as regular cookies do, so you need to flatten them. Make them look as deceptively cookie-like as possible.

4 Bake the trick cookies for about 15 minutes, until slightly golden brown. Use oven mitts to remove the cookies from the oven. Let them cool on the pan for a couple of minutes, and then use the metal spatula to transfer them to the cooling rack. Put the rubber band around the handle of the spray-thingy on the sink, and remind your brother to wash his hands before eating.

The deliciously cheesy smell of these fake-out cookies could alert your family to the prank. What to do? Scent the kitchen with the more cookie-like aroma of hot cider. Just pour some apple cider in a pot, toss in a couple cinnamon sticks, and heat the pot on the stove on the lowest setting.

Egg-cellent Cookies

Making these gorgeous, cake-like cookies is like doing an art project. They're almost too pretty to eat.

Yield: about 20 eggs

equipment

- measuring cups and spoons
- 2 mixing bowls
- electric mixer
- cookie sheet, lined with parchment paper
- spoon
- whisk
- 4-6 small dishes
- plastic wrap
- oven mitts
- metal spatula
- wire cooling rack
- waxed paper
- several pastry bags (page 15)

ingredients

- 1 stick ($\frac{1}{2}$ cup) butter, softened
- 1 cup sugar
- 2 eggs
- $\frac{1}{2}$ teaspoon vanilla extract
- $\frac{1}{2}$ cup milk
- $2\frac{1}{4}$ cups flour, sifted
- $\frac{1}{2}$ teaspoon baking powder
- $\frac{1}{4}$ teaspoon salt
- 2 pounds (8 cups) powdered sugar
- $\frac{1}{4}$ cup light corn syrup
- 1 teaspoon vanilla extract
- $\frac{1}{2}$ cup very hot water
- food coloring

1 Preheat the oven to 375°F. Cream the butter and sugar. Add the eggs and $\frac{1}{2}$ teaspoon of vanilla extract. Beat until well blended.

2 Add the milk and mix. Add the flour, baking powder, and salt. Mix on low speed until the flour is moistened. Then beat until you have fluffy batter. Let it rest for 10 minutes.

3 Glop spoonfuls of batter far apart on the parchment-lined cookie sheet. Use the back of the spoon to smooth the glops into egg-shapes. Bake the cookies for 12 to 14 minutes. Meahwhile, combine the powdered sugar, corn syrup, 1 teaspoon of vanilla extract, and hot water in a mixing bowl. Whisk until smooth. This icing is called poured fondant.

4 Divide the fondant among the small dishes. Make each batch a different color by adding food coloring a drop at a time. Cover each dish with plastic wrap touching the icing. Put the dishes on the warm stove. (Fondant dries quickly. It pours best when warm.)

5 Use oven mitts to remove the cookies from the oven. Use the metal spatula to move them to the wire rack. Lay a sheet of waxed paper under the rack to catch drips. When they're cool, coat each egg with fondant. Spoon the rest of the icing into waxed paper pastry bags. Let your creative genius take over as you draw on your eggs.

equipment

- measuring cups and spoons
- 3 mixing bowls
- electric mixer
- plastic wrap
- lightly floured pastry board
- rolling pin
- round cookie cutter
- greased cookie sheet
- metal spatula
- wire cooling rack

Yield: 2 dozen planets

ingredients

- 2 sticks (1 cup) butter, softened
- 1½ cups sugar
- 2 eggs
- 1 tablespoon vanilla extract
- 3 cups flour
- ½ teaspoon salt
- food coloring

Earth Day
April 22

Planet Earth

Celebrate our big, beautiful world with Earth-look-alike cookies. Devour the cookies, but give our natural resources a break!

1 Cream the butter and sugar. Add the eggs and vanilla extract. Beat until well blended.

2 Mix the flour and salt into the butter mixture. Blend well. Divide the dough into three bowls. Color one batch green and one blue, working the color into the dough with your fingers. Leave the third white. Chill the dough for at least 15 minutes.

3 Preheat the oven to 375°F. Squish the three colors of dough together a little bit. Don't over-squish, or you'll make a new color instead of swirls. Wrap half of the dough in plastic wrap, mash it into a disc, and stick it in the fridge.

4 Sprinkle flour on the rolling pin. Working with the dough that isn't in the fridge, roll the dough out to about ¼ inch thick. Cut circles so these cookies will look like the Earth as viewed from outer space.

5 Place the cookies 1 inch apart on the greased cookie sheet. Bake 8 to 10 minutes. Use oven mitts to remove the cookies from the oven. Use the metal spatula to move the hot cookies to the cooling rack.

6 Repeat steps 4 and 5 with the remaining dough. Don't waste the scrap dough! Squish all of your dough scraps together, wrap and chill them, and repeat steps 4 and 5 again.

Peanut Butter & Chocolate Buckeyes

Go out and plant a tree. Then reward yourself with a batch of these. They look like the nut of—you guessed it—the buckeye tree.

Yield: about 30 buckeyes

equipment

- measuring cups
- mixing bowl
- wooden spoon
- microwave-safe bowl (not metal)
- spoon
- 2 forks (If you have a fondue set, use a pair of those forks.)
- cookie sheet lined with parchment or waxed paper

ingredients

- 1 cup peanut butter
- 1 cup powdered milk
- ½ cup honey
- ⅔ cup powdered sugar
- 4-ounce bar of semi-sweet chocolate, broken into chocolate chip-sized pieces
- 1 teaspoon cooking oil

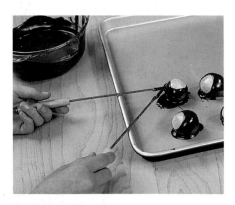

1 Combine the peanut butter, powdered milk, honey, and powdered sugar in the bowl. Stir until evenly blended. If your stirring arm gets tired, you can finish mixing with your hands. Roll the dough between your palms into balls about the size of a shooter marble. Refrigerate the peanut butter balls for at least 20 minutes, until firm.

2 Put the chocolate in the microwave-safe bowl. Microwave it on medium power for 2 minutes. Stir the oil into the chocolate. If the mixture isn't smooth, microwave it for 30 seconds. Stir again.

3 Use the fork to dip a peanut butter ball ¾ of the way into the chocolate. Make sure to dip the fork, too, so the holes won't show. Push the buckeye off of the fork and onto the lined cookie sheet. (See photo at left.) Repeat with the rest of the peanut butter balls.

4 The cookie sheet is kind of a fake-out. You don't bake these cookies. They're ready for eating!

equipment

- measuring cups and spoons
- mixing bowl
- electric mixer
- spoon
- greased cookie sheet
- oven mitts
- metal spatula
- lunch-sized paper bag

Yield: about 40 little cookies

ingredients

- 2 sticks (1 cup) butter, softened
- 1/2 cup powdered sugar, plus a little extra
- 1 teaspoon vanilla extract
- 2 cups flour
- 1/4 teaspoon salt
- 1/2 cup chopped pecans (optional)

Cinco de Mayo
May 5

Mexican Wedding Cookies

Celebrate Mexico's Independence Day with these delicioso cookies. Just one batch makes plenty to share, so practice saying, "de nada."

1 Preheat the oven to 350°F. Cream the butter and 1/2 cup of powdered sugar. Add the vanilla extract. Beat until combined. Add the flour and salt, and mix until you have dough. Mix in the pecans until evenly distributed.

2 Use your clean hands to roll small spoonfuls of dough into balls. The cookies spread in the oven, so make the balls smaller than you want the finished cookies to be. Place the dough balls on the greased cookie sheet.

3 Bake 20 to 25 minutes (less for really tiny cookies) until slightly brown at the edges and dry on top. Use oven mitts to remove the cookies from the oven.

4 Put about 1/2 cup of powdered sugar in the paper bag. Transfer the warm cookies to the bag and shake it up. Be gentle—the goal is to have sugar-coated cookies, not sugar mixed with crumbs.

Q-Busy's Favorites

My mom's hip hop name is Q-Busy. No, she doesn't rap, but she is busy. Anyway, I'm sure your mom will love these chewy cookies as much as mine does.

equipment

- measuring cups and spoons
- mixing bowl
- electric mixer
- wooden spoon
- spoon
- greased cookie sheet
- oven mitts
- metal spatula
- wire cooling rack

Yield: 3 to 4 dozen cookies, depending on how big you make them

ingredients

- 2 sticks (1 cup) butter, softened
- 2/3 cup sugar
- 2/3 cup (packed) brown sugar
- 2 eggs
- 2 teaspoons vanilla extract
- 1 1/2 cups flour
- 1 teaspoon baking soda
- 1/2 teaspoon salt
- 1/2 teaspoon ground nutmeg
- 1 1/2 cups quick oats (not old fashioned or instant oatmeal)
- 2/3 cup pecan pieces
- 2/3 cup dried cranberries
- 1 cup chocolate chips
- 1 to 2 tablespoons orange zest

1 Preheat the oven to 375°F. Cream the butter, sugar, and brown sugar. Add the eggs and vanilla extract. Beat until the ingredients are well blended.

2 Add the flour, baking soda, salt, and nutmeg to the butter mixture. Mix until you don't see any streaks of flour.

3 Add the oats, pecans, cranberries, chocolate chips, and zest. Use the wooden spoon to stir the dough until all the goodies are evenly distributed.

4 Spoon the dough onto the greased cookie sheet, leaving a couple inches between each cookie. Bake for 8 to 10 minutes.

5 Use oven mitts to remove the cookies from the oven. Use the metal spatula to move the hot cookies to the cooling rack. Instead of just cleaning up your cookie mess, clean the kitchen all the way. Your mom deserves it!

equipment

- measuring cups and spoons
- mixing bowl
- paper towel
- electric mixer
- rubber spatula
- spoon
- cookie sheet lined with parchment paper
- oven mitts
- wire cooling rack

Yield: about 2 dozen macaroons

ingredients

- 1 teaspoon of vinegar
- 3 egg whites (page 12)
- ¼ cup sugar
- 3 tablespoons cornstarch
- ¼ cup candied ginger, chopped
- 2 cups sweetened coconut flakes

Memorial Day
May 31

Coconut Ginger Macaroons

The fluffy texture and tropical flavors of these cookies make them the perfect dessert for the first picnic or barbeque of the year.

1 Preheat the oven to 350°F. Wipe the inside of your mixing bowl with a vinegary paper towel. (The bowl should still look dry. This is the trick for whipping egg whites.) Pour the egg whites into the clean bowl. Gradually add the sugar and cornstarch to the whites as you whip on high speed. Whip until the mixture resembles shaving cream.

2 Fold the ginger and coconut into the egg whites with the spatula. Spoon dollops of the mixture onto the parchment-lined cookie sheet. Bake 15 to 18 minutes, until browned.

3 Use oven mitts to remove the cookies from the oven. While still wearing the mitts, drag the parchment paper onto the cooling rack. When the macaroons are cool, peel them off of the paper.

Jelly-Filled Thumbprints

I have my father's hands. (In a jar. Wanna see?) No, really, I inherited the perfect thumbs for making these cookies. Thanks, Papa!

equipment

- measuring cups and spoons
- mixing bowl
- electric mixer
- greased cookie sheet
- spoon
- oven mitts
- metal spatula
- wire cooling rack

Yield: 3 to 4 dozen cookies

ingredients

- 2 sticks (1 cup) butter, softened
- 1 1/2 cups sugar
- 2 eggs
- 1 tablespoon vanilla extract
- 3 cups flour
- 1/2 teaspoon salt
- 1 to 2 teaspoons ground cinnamon, nutmeg, or lemon zest (Choose one that goes well with the jam you're using.)
- powdered sugar
- your dad's favorite jam (Mine likes cherry preserves.)

1 Cream the butter and sugar. Add the eggs and vanilla extract. Beat until well blended.

2 Mix the flour, salt, and spice or zest into the butter mixture. Blend the ingredients well. Chill the cookie dough for at least 15 minutes.

3 Preheat the oven to 375°F. Rub powdered sugar on the palms of your clean hands. Roll balls of dough about the size of a huge gumball. Use more powdered sugar if things get too sticky.

4 Place the balls about 1 inch apart on the cookie sheet. Use your thumb to press an indentation in each cookie. Fill the indentations with jam.

5 Bake these cookies for 8 to 10 minutes, until slightly golden around the bottom edges. Use oven mitts to remove the cookies from the oven. Let the cookies cool on the pan for a couple of minutes. Use the spatula to transfer the warm cookies to the cooling rack.

equipment

- measuring cups and spoons
- food processor
- 9 x 13-inch baking dish, greased
- fork
- mixing bowl
- whisk
- oven mitts
- sifter

Yield: 15 squares of lemony goodness

ingredients

- 2 cups flour
- $\frac{1}{2}$ cup powdered sugar, plus extra for garnish
- 2 sticks (1 cup) butter, cut into chunks
- 4 eggs
- 2 cups sugar
- $\frac{1}{4}$ cup flour
- $\frac{1}{2}$ teaspoon baking powder
- $\frac{1}{4}$ teaspoon salt
- 1 tablespoon lemon zest
- $\frac{1}{2}$ cup lemon juice (from 2 or 3 lemons)

Summer Solstice

June 21 (Northern Hemisphere)

Lemon Squares

These sunny cookies are just right for the longest day of the year. See if you can wake up at sunrise and stay outdoors until sunset. Don't forget sunscreen!

1 Preheat the oven to 350°F. Put the 2 cups of flour, $\frac{1}{2}$ cup of powdered sugar, and butter in the food processor. Process the ingredients until they come together as a ball of dough. Press the dough into the baking dish, and prick it all over with the fork. Bake 20 minutes.

2 While the crust is baking, make the lemon filling. Break the eggs into the mixing bowl and whisk until your arm gets tired. Add the sugar, $\frac{1}{4}$ cup flour, baking powder, and salt. Whisk until all the lumps dissolve. Whisk in the zest and juice until evenly blended.

3 Pour the lemon mixture over the baked crust. Bake another 25 to 30 minutes, until slightly brown at the edges. Use oven mitts to remove the baked food from the oven. Now the hard part: wait for it to cool before cutting it into squares. Sift powdered sugar on top.

Frosted Maple Leaves

These cookies are as tasty as they are beautiful. They look like the Canadian flag, eh?

Yield: 3 to 4 dozen leaves, depending on the size of your cookie cutter

ingredients

- 2 sticks (1 cup) butter, softened
- 1½ cups sugar
- 2 eggs
- 1 tablespoon vanilla extract
- 3 cups flour
- ½ teaspoon salt

- 1 pound (4 cups) powdered sugar
- ½ cup milk
- 1 teaspoon maple extract
- red food coloring (Professional cake decorating paste, found at craft stores, makes the best red.)
- ½ recipe Royal Icing (page 15)

equipment

- measuring cups and spoons
- 2 mixing bowls
- electric mixer
- plastic wrap
- lightly floured pastry board
- rolling pin
- maple leaf-shaped cookie cutter
- greased cookie sheet
- whisk
- pastry bag (page 15)
- oven mitts
- metal spatula
- wire cooling rack
- waxed paper
- spoon

1 Cream the butter and sugar. Add the eggs and vanilla extract. Beat until well blended.

2 Add the flour and salt. Blend well. Divide the dough in half. Wrap each half in plastic wrap. Mash them into discs about ½ inch thick. Chill for at least 15 minutes.

3 Preheat the oven to 375°F. Sprinkle flour on the rolling pin. Roll each disc out to about ¼ inch thick. Use the cookie cutter to cut out maple leaf shapes. Squish the dough scraps together. Repeat the wrapping, mashing, chilling, rolling, and cutting.

4 Place the leaves 1 inch apart on the greased cookie sheet. Bake these cookies for 8 to 10 minutes. While the cookies bake, whisk the powdered sugar, milk, maple extract, and a bit of food coloring together to make a red glaze. Put the Royal Icing in your pastry bag.

5 Use oven mitts to remove the cookies from the oven. Let the cookies cool on the pan for a couple of minutes. Use the spatula to move the cookies to the wire rack. Lay waxed paper under the rack. Outline the cooled cookies with the icing. Spoon glaze inside the outline.

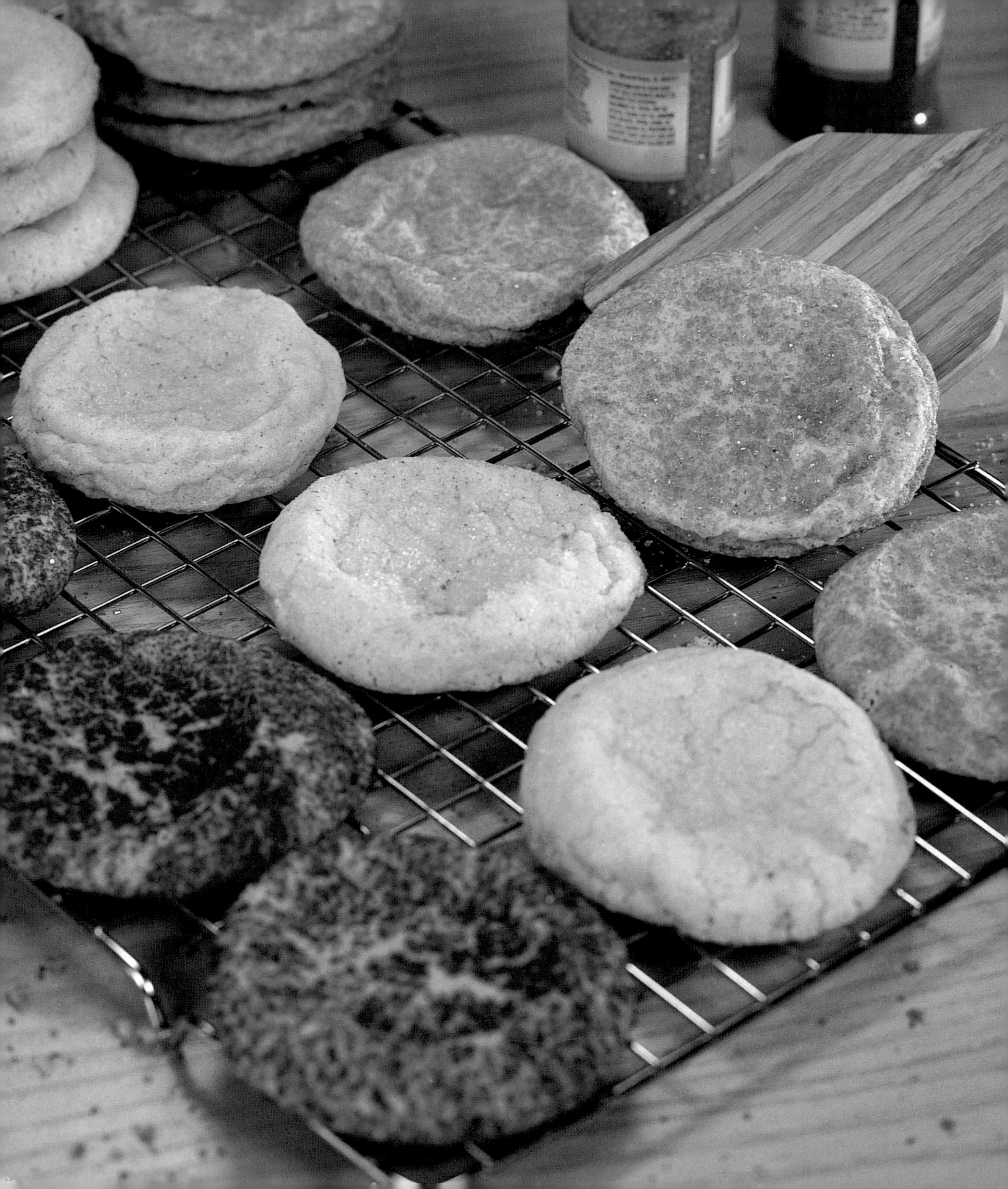

equipment

- measuring cups and spoons
- mixing bowl
- electric mixer
- rubber spatula
- 3 shallow dishes
- spoon
- greased cookie sheet
- oven mitts
- metal spatula
- wire cooling rack

Yield: about 3 dozen snickerdoodles

ingredients

- 2 sticks (1 cup) butter, softened
- 2 cups sugar
- 2 eggs
- 2 teaspoons vanilla extract
- 3 cups flour
- 2 teaspoons cream of tartar
- 1 teaspoon baking soda
- 1/4 teaspoon salt
- 1 teaspoon ground cinnamon
- red, white, and blue sparkle sugar (Use regular sugar for slightly less patriotic cookies.)

U.S. Independence Day
July 4

Snickerdoodle Dandies

Celebrate the signing of the United States Declaration of Independence by exercising your inalienable rights to life, liberty, and the pursuit of cookies.

1 Preheat the oven to 350°F. Cream the butter and sugar. Add the eggs and vanilla extract. Beat until well blended.

2 Scrape down the sides of the bowl with the rubber spatula. Add the flour, cream of tartar, baking soda, salt, and cinnamon. Mix until the ingredients are combined.

3 Put a few tablespoons of each sparkle sugar into a dish. Roll a spoonful of dough between your palms into a ball about the size of a shooter marble. Roll the dough ball in sugar to coat it.

4 Place the cookie on the greased cookie sheet. Make more sugarcoated cookies with the rest of the dough. These cookies spread a lot, so give them plenty of space on the cookie sheet.

5 Bake the snickerdoodles 10 to 12 minutes, until the tops are craggy and slightly puffed. Use oven mitts to remove the cookies from the oven. Leave them on the pan for a couple minutes to cool. Then, use the metal spatula to move the cookies to the wire rack to finish cooling.

Dunkable Palmiers

Just one bite of these crispy, palm-shaped cookies will make you exclaim "Viva la France!"

equipment

- measuring cups and spoons
- mixing bowl
- pastry board
- rolling pin
- sharp knife
- greased cookie sheet
- oven mitts
- metal spatula
- wire cooling rack

Yield: 2 dozen cookies

ingredients

- 1 pound frozen puff pastry, thawed according to the package directions
- ⅔ cup sugar, divided
- ½ teaspoon ground cinnamon, divided

1 There are two sheets of puff pastry in the package. You'll work with one sheet at a time, using half the sugar per sheet. Stir ¼ teaspoon cinnamon into ⅓ cup of sugar.

2 Sprinkle half of the mixture on your pastry board. Unfold a sheet of puff pastry. Lay it on top of the cinnamon-sugar. Sprinkle the rest of the mixture on top of the pastry.

3 Roll the pastry out into a rectangle about ⅛ inch thick. Fold the long sides of dough in toward the middle of the rectangle, leaving about a ½-inch gap. Next, fold the dough in half so that the short sides match up. (The top photo shows this mid-step.) Feel for the dent where you left that gap. Fold the dough along the dent. (See the bottom photo.) Chill the dough for at least 30 minutes. Meanwhile, repeat steps 1, 2, and 3 with the other sheet of puff pastry.

4 Preheat the oven to 425°F. Cut the chilled dough into ¼-inch slices. Place the slices a few inches apart on the greased cookie sheet. Bake 6 to 8 minutes, until the edges are golden brown. Use oven mitts to take the cookies out of the oven. Use the metal spatula to flip them over. Bake for another 2 to 3 minutes.

5 Use the metal spatula to move the palmiers onto the wire rack to cool. Bon appétit!

equipment

- measuring cups and spoons
- mixing bowl
- electric mixer
- plastic wrap
- lightly floured pastry board
- rolling pin
- round cookie cutter
- greased cookie sheet
- metal spatula
- wire cooling rack
- ice cream scoop

yield: about a dozen sandwiches

ingredients

- 1 stick ($\frac{1}{2}$ cup) butter, softened
- $\frac{3}{4}$ cup sugar
- 1 egg
- $1\frac{1}{4}$ cups flour
- $\frac{1}{3}$ cup cocoa powder
- $\frac{1}{4}$ teaspoon baking soda
- $\frac{1}{8}$ teaspoon salt
- your favorite ice cream

National Ice Cream Day (United States)
July 15

Ice Cream Sandwiches

Now here's a holiday we can all celebrate wholeheartedly. I scream! You scream! We all scream for ice cream!

1 Cream the butter and sugar. Add the egg. Beat until well blended.

2 Mix the flour, cocoa powder, baking soda, and salt into the butter mixture. Blend well. Divide the dough in half. Wrap each half in plastic wrap, and mash them into discs about $\frac{1}{2}$ inch thick. Chill the cookie dough for at least 20 minutes.

3 Preheat the oven to 350°F. Sprinkle flour on the rolling pin. Working with one disc of chilled dough at a time, roll the dough out to between $\frac{1}{4}$ and $\frac{1}{8}$ inch thick. Use the cookie cutter to cut out circles. Squish the dough scraps together. Repeat all the wrapping, mashing, chilling, rolling, and cutting with the scraps.

4 Place the cookies 1 inch apart on the greased cookie sheet. Bake these cookies for 10 to 12 minutes. Use oven mitts to remove the cookies from the oven. Let the baked cookies cool on the pan for a couple of minutes. Then use the spatula to transfer the warm cookies to the cooling rack.

5 Put scoops of ice cream between two cookies, and mash the sandwich together. Yum!

Applesauce for the Teacher

Everyone knows that teachers like apples. They also like cookies. Combine the two and what do you get? Chewy cookies and a smile!

equipment

- measuring cups and spoons
- mixing bowl
- fork
- wooden spoon
- greased cookie sheet
- spoon
- oven mitts
- metal spatula
- wire cooling rack

Yield: about 2 dozen cookies

ingredients

- 1 cup applesauce
- 2 eggs
- $\frac{1}{2}$ cup vegetable oil
- 1 teaspoon vanilla extract
- 1 cup flour
- 1 teaspoon ground cinnamon
- 1 teaspoon baking soda
- $\frac{1}{2}$ teaspoon salt
- 1 cup quick oats (not old-fashioned or instant)
- $1\frac{1}{2}$ cups goodies, such as nuts, raisins, or chocolate chips

1 Preheat the oven to 375°F. Add the applesauce, eggs, oil, and vanilla extract to the mixing bowl. Use the fork to lightly beat the ingredients until they're well combined.

2 Add the flour, cinnamon, baking soda, salt, and oats. Stir with the wooden spoon until the dry ingredients are moistened. Add the goodies (I used slivered almonds, golden raisins, and toffee chips in mine). Stir until evenly distributed.

3 Spoon glops of dough 1-inch apart on the greased cookie sheet. Bake 8 to 10 minutes. Use oven mitts to remove the cookies from the oven.

4 Let the hot cookies rest a couple of minutes. Then use the metal spatula to transfer them to the cooling rack. Now the hard part: do you give all the cookies to your favorite teacher, or divide them evenly among all of your teachers? You may need to snack on a cookie to help you think this through.

equipment

- measuring cups
- mixing bowl
- electric mixer
- pastry board
- rolling pin
- bone-shaped cookie cutter
- greased cookie sheet

Yield: about 2 dozen dog treats

ingredients

- 3 eggs
- $1/2$ cup milk
- $1/4$ cup cooking oil
- $1/4$ cup molasses (Lightly grease the measuring cup so the molasses doesn't stick.)
- $2^2/3$ cups whole-wheat flour

Dog Days
August

Give a Dog a Bone

Sirius, the Dog Star, is in the sky during the late summer in the Northern Hemisphere. Celebrate this sweltering time of year by making cookies for your four-legged friends.

1 Preheat the oven to 350°F. Mix the eggs, milk, oil, and molasses until well combined. Add the flour. Mix on low speed until the flour is moistened. Then work the dough with your hands, mixing until the dough comes together in a ball.

2 Let the dough rest at room temperature for 10 to 15 minutes. Then, roll the dough out to $1/4$ inch thick. Use the cookie cutter to cut out doggie bones.

3 Place the bones about $1/2$ inch apart on the greased cookie sheet. Bake for 30 minutes. Want extra-crunchy treats that are good for your dog's teeth? Turn the oven off, but leave the cookies in for another 30 minutes. Use oven mitts to remove the cookies from the oven.

4 Let the treats cool before you give one to your dog. (You could ask him to do a trick first!) Overeating a new treat can upset canine tummies, so don't feed your dog more than two cookies a day.

Labor Day
September (America), May (Europe)

Take-It-Easy Cookies

How do we celebrate workers and their efforts to make workplaces safe and jobs secure? By taking a day off, of course! (These delicious cookies require very little work.)

Yield: about 3 dozen cookies

ingredients

- 1½ sticks (¾ cup) butter
- 3 cups sugar
- ¾ cup milk
- 4½ cups old-fashioned or quick oats (not instant oatmeal)
- 1½ cups chocolate chips
- 1½ teaspoons vanilla extract

1 Put the butter in the pot. Rub the butter wrappers on the inside of the pot, greasing the sides. This will prevent boiling-over disasters.

2 Add the sugar and milk to the pot. Bring the concoction to a boil over medium heat. Let it boil for exactly 1 minute, and then remove the pot from the burner. (Don't forget to turn off the stove.)

3 Add the oats, chocolate chips, and vanilla extract. Stir the mixture until the chips are melted and the oats are coated.

4 Plop spoonfuls of the mixture onto waxed paper. Don't touch—it's hotter than it looks. Let the cookies cool for about 20 minutes, until they're hard.

equipment

- measuring cups and spoons
- mixing bowl
- electric mixer
- rubber spatula
- greased cookie sheet
- spoon
- oven mitts
- metal spatula
- wire cooling rack

Yield: about 2 dozen cookies

ingredients

- 1 stick ($1/2$ cup) butter, softened
- $3/4$ cup (packed) brown sugar
- 1 egg
- $1/2$ cup molasses (Lightly grease the measuring cup so the molasses doesn't stick.)
- 2 cups flour
- $1/2$ teaspoon baking soda
- $1/4$ teaspoon salt
- $1/2$ teaspoon ground cinnamon
- $1/2$ teaspoon ground ginger

Talk Like a Pirate Day
September 19

Arrr-some Molassies

Shiver me timbers! These arrr the best cookies on the seven seas! Make a batch for ye mateys.

1 Preheat the oven to 350°F. Cream the butter and brown sugar. Add the egg and molasses. Beat until smooth and lighter in color.

2 Scrape down the sides of the bowl with the rubber spatula. Add the flour, baking soda, salt, cinnamon, and ginger. Mix until the ingredients are well blended.

3 Drop spoonfuls of dough a couple of inches apart on the greased cookie sheet. Bake for 10 to 12 minutes, until the tops are dry-looking and slightly puffed.

4 Use oven mitts to remove the cookies from the oven. Leave them on the pan for a couple of minutes to cool. Then, use the metal spatula to move the cookies to the wire rack to finish cooling. Share your booty with your most swashbuckling friends.

Ginger Orange Lace

These crispy cookies look like autumn leaves—and they crackle and crunch in your mouth.

Yield: about 2 dozen cookies

equipment

- measuring cups and spoons
- small saucepot
- whisk
- 2 spoons
- greased cookie sheet
- oven mitts
- metal spatula
- rolling pin
- coffee mugs (optional)

ingredients

- $1/2$ stick ($1/4$ cup) butter
- $1/4$ cup sugar
- 1 tablespoon molasses
- 1 tablespoon corn syrup
- 1 teaspoon vanilla extract
- $1/2$ cup flour, sifted
- $1/8$ teaspoon salt
- 1 teaspoon fresh grated ginger
- $1/2$ teaspoon orange zest

Note: If you don't have molasses, double the amount of corn syrup. The cookies will be lighter in color, with smaller holes, like the bottom cookie in the photo.

1 Preheat the oven to 350°F. Melt the butter, sugar, molasses, and corn syrup in the pot over medium-low heat. Whisk the concoction until blended. (The butter will separate out a bit, but that's no big deal.)

2 Add the vanilla extract, flour, salt, ginger, and orange zest. Whisk until the whole mixture is the consistency of caramel sauce.

3 Spoon about 2 teaspoons of dough far apart on the cookie sheet. The mixture is hot, so use a second spoon to push it off the first spoon. Only spoon out six per sheet.

4 Bake the crisps for 5 to 7 minutes. Each cookie should be lacy all the way through, and the color should be lighter than the dough, even in the middle.

5 Use oven mitts to remove the cookies from the oven. Let the baked cookies rest on the pan for about 1 minute, until you can get the metal spatula under a cookie without wrinkling it. Drape the warm cookies over the rolling pin to shape them. If you run out of room on the rolling pin, use coffee mugs.

equipment

- measuring cups and spoons
- mixing bowl
- electric mixer
- well-greased 9 x 13 baking dish
- oven mitts
- small saucepot
- paring knife
- metal spatula

Yield: 3 dozen little cakes

ingredients

- 1 stick ($\frac{1}{2}$ cup) butter, softened
- $\frac{1}{2}$ cup sugar
- 1 cup plain yogurt
- $1\frac{1}{2}$ cups semolina flour
- 1 teaspoon baking powder
- 18 blanched almonds, split in half lengthwise
- $\frac{1}{2}$ cup honey
- 1 cup sugar
- $\frac{1}{2}$ cup water
- 1 tablespoon rose water

'Id al-Fitr
October (advances annually)

Basboosa

Mmm. If you've never tried these honey cakes, you're in for a treat. If I ever feast after a fast, these will be on the menu.

1 Cream the butter and $\frac{1}{2}$ cup sugar. Add the yogurt. Beat until combined. Add the semolina flour and baking powder, and mix until you have sticky dough. Let this dough rest for 30 minutes.

2 Preheat the oven to 375°F. Use your clean hands to pat the dough into the baking dish. Bake 20 minutes. Use oven mitts to take the dish out of the oven. Cut the partially-baked dough into diamonds. Press half of an almond onto each diamond. Return the basboosa to the oven, and bake an additional 10 to 15 minutes.

3 While the cakes bake, combine the honey, 1 cup sugar, water, and rose water in the pot. Cook over low heat until the mixture is the thickness of syrup. When you're ready for step 4, turn off the stove.

4 Use the oven mitts to remove the cookies from the oven. Pour the syrup all over the hot basboosa. Now the hard part: wait for the baking dish to cool to room temperature. Take the cakes out of the dish with the metal spatula.

Halloween
October 31

Ghostly Kisses

Beware the chocolaty ghosties! They look cute, but they're spooky—just watch them disappear.

equipment
- paper towel
- mixing bowl
- 2 cookie sheets lined with parchment paper
- measuring cups and spoons
- electric mixer
- rubber spatula
- large cloth pastry bag

Yield: about 20 ghosts

ingredients
- 1 teaspoon vinegar
- about 20 chocolate kisses
- 3 egg whites (page 12), at room temperature
- 1/2 teaspoon cream of tartar
- 1 1/2 cups sugar
- mini chocolate chips

1 Preheat the oven to 375°F. Wipe out the inside of the mixing bowl with a vinegary paper towel. (This is the trick for whipping egg whites.) Unwrap the chocolate kisses, and arrange them on the cookie sheets.

2 Beat the egg whites with the cream of tartar until foamy. Turn the mixer up to high. Gradually add the sugar while you whip the egg whites. This concoction is called meringue. Keep whipping until the meringue is bright-white and glossy. Turn off the mixer, and lift the beaters. Does the meringue form a peak that flops over just a little at the top? If so, move on to the next step. If the whole peak flops over, whip it some more.

3 You don't need a tip for your pastry bag to make these ghosts. Use a rubber spatula to fill the bag with meringue. (You'll probably have better luck just using half of the meringue at a time, even if all of it could fit.) Gently squeeze ghostly bodies and heads over the chocolate kisses. Don't worry if your first few ghosts look blobby—you'll get the hang of it!

4 Press mini chocolate chips point-first into the ghosts' faces for eyes. Put the cookie sheets in the oven. TURN OFF THE OVEN IMMEDIATELY. Leave the ghosties in the oven for 3 hours. No peeking! You might want to put a note on the oven to make sure no one else in your family turns it on or opens the door. By the time you've got your costume on, the ghosts will be ready to haunt your mouth.

equipment

- measuring cups and spoons
- mixing bowl
- electric mixer
- spoon
- shallow dish
- greased cookie sheet
- oven mitts
- metal spatula

Yield: about 3 dozen little cookies

ingredients

- 2 sticks (1 cup) butter, softened
- 1 cup powdered sugar
- 1 teaspoon vanilla extract
- 2¼ cups flour
- 1 teaspoon ground cardamom
- ½ cup chopped cashews
- about ⅓ cup finely shredded coconut

Diwali
October or November

Cashew Cardamom Coconut Cookies

Break out the candles and sparklers! You can make these Indian cookies look extra-festive by sprinkling purple sparkle-sugar on them.

1 Preheat the oven to 350°F. Cream the butter and sugar. Add the vanilla extract. Blend. Add the flour and cardamom. Mix until you have dough. Mix in the cashews until evenly distributed.

2 Pour the coconut into the shallow dish. Use your clean hands to roll small spoonfuls of dough into balls. Roll the balls in the coconut to coat them. Place the balls on the greased cookie sheet.

3 Bake 20 to 25 minutes until the coconut is toasted. Use oven mitts to remove the cookies from the oven. Let the cookies cool for a couple of minutes on the pan, and then use the metal spatula to move them to the wire rack to finish cooling.

Day of the Dead/All Saints' Day/All Souls' Day
November 1 and 2

Zany Skulls

Ain't no sin to take off your skin and dance around in your bones!

Yield: 3 to 4 dozen skulls, depending on the size of your cookie cutter

ingredients

- 2 sticks (1 cup) butter, softened
- 1½ cups sugar
- 2 eggs
- 1 tablespoon vanilla extract
- 3 cups flour
- ½ teaspoon salt
- egg wash (page 14)
- Buttercream Frosting (page 15)
- food coloring
- cocoa powder

equipment

- measuring cups and spoons
- 3 mixing bowls
- electric mixer
- plastic wrap
- lightly floured pastry board
- rolling pin
- oval cookie cutter
- paring knife
- greased cookie sheet
- oven mitts
- metal spatula
- wire cooling rack
- rubber spatula
- 2 pastry bags (page 15)

1 Cream the butter and sugar. Add the eggs and vanilla extract. Beat well. Add the flour and salt. Blend well.

2 Divide the dough in half. Wrap each half in plastic wrap. Mash them into discs. Chill the cookie dough for at least 15 minutes.

3 Preheat the oven to 375°F. Sprinkle flour on the rolling pin. Roll each dough disc out to about ¼ inch thick. Use the cookie cutter to cut out oval crania. Use the paring knife to make square jaws and triangular bows. Stick the shapes together with egg wash. (See page 14.)

4 Place the skulls 1 inch apart on the greased cookie sheet. Bake for 8 to 10 minutes. Use oven mitts to remove the cookies from the oven. Let the cookies cool before using the spatula to transfer them to the wire rack.

5 Use the rubber spatula to frost all the cookies white. Divide the remaining frosting in half. Add food coloring to one half for the bows. Add cocoa powder to the other half, one teaspoon at a time, until you get a dark color for the eye sockets, eyebrows, and mouths. Use pastry bags to decorate the cooled cookies. Laugh maniacally as you crunch skulls between your teeth.

equipment

- measuring cups and spoons
- mixing bowl
- electric mixer
- plastic wrap
- lightly floured pastry board
- rolling pin
- round cookie cutter
- greased cookie sheet
- oven mitts
- metal spatula
- wire cooling rack

Yield: about 2 dozen poppies, depending on the size of your cookie cutter

ingredients

- 2 sticks (1 cup) butter, softened
- 1½ cups sugar
- 2 eggs
- 1 tablespoon vanilla extract
- 3 cups flour
- ½ teaspoon salt
- red food coloring (Professional cake decorators' paste, found in craft stores, makes the richest red.)
- egg wash (page 14)
- a couple tablespoons of poppy seeds

Pretty Poppies

We honor the sacrifices made by all people who have been in the armed forces. The poppy is this holiday's symbol because of the poem "In Flanders Fields" by John McCrae.

1 Cream the butter and sugar. Add the eggs and vanilla extract. Beat until well blended. Mix the flour and salt into the butter mixture. Set aside a quarter of the dough. Add red food coloring to the rest. Blend until the dough is evenly red.

2 Divide the dough in half. Wrap each half in plastic wrap, and mash them into discs about ½ inch thick. Chill the cookie dough for at least 15 minutes.

3 Preheat the oven to 375°F. Sprinkle flour on the rolling pin. Working with one disc of chilled dough at a time, roll the dough out to about ¼ inch thick. Use the cookie cutter to cut out round flower petals.

4 Use egg wash to glue five petals together for each flower. Roll a bit of uncolored dough into a ball. Cover this ball in egg wash, and then roll it in poppy seeds. Press the seed-covered ball flat in the center of a flower. Repeat for each flower.

5 Place the poppies 1 inch apart on the greased cookie sheet. Bake these cookies for 8 to 10 minutes. Use oven mitts to remove the cookies from the oven. Let the cookies cool on the pan for a couple of minutes. Use the spatula to transfer the warm cookies to the cooling rack.

Thanksgiving
Autumn (varies by country)

Pumpkin Puffs

Is your Thanksgiving all about dinner? Start a new tradition: muffin-like breakfast cookies!

Yield: 2 dozen cookies

equipment

- measuring cups and spoons
- 2 mixing bowls
- electric mixer
- 2 spoons
- greased cookie sheet
- drinking glass
- whisk
- oven mitts
- metal spatula
- wire cooling rack
- waxed paper

ingredients

- 1 stick (½ cup) butter, softened
- 1 cup (packed) brown sugar
- ½ cup sugar, plus a little extra
- 1 egg
- 15-ounce can of pumpkin (not pumpkin pie filling)
- 1 teaspoon vanilla extract
- 2 cups flour
- ¾ teaspoon baking soda
- ¼ teaspoon salt
- 1 teaspoon ground cinnamon
- ½ teaspoon ground ginger
- ⅛ teaspoon ground cloves
- 1 pound (4 cups) powdered sugar
- ½ cup milk
- ¾ teaspoon maple extract
- walnut chips

1 Preheat the oven to 375°F. Cream the butter, brown sugar, and ½ cup sugar. Add the egg, pumpkin, and vanilla extract. Beat.

2 Add the flour, baking soda, salt, and spices to the pumpkin mixture. Mix on low until just combined.

3 Drop spoonfuls of dough a couple of inches apart on the greased cookie sheet. Since this dough is goopy, push it off the spoon with another spoon. Then rub a little dough on the bottom of the glass to moisten it. Press the glass into a little bit of sugar. Use the sugarcoated glass to flatten the dough globs just a bit. Re-sugar the glass as needed.

4 Bake the cookies for 10 to 12 minutes. While the cookies are baking, whisk the powdered sugar, milk, and maple extract together to make a glaze.

5 Use oven mitts to take the cookies out of the oven. Let them cool on the pan for a couple minutes, and then use the metal spatula to move them to the cooling rack. Put some waxed paper under the rack to catch drips. Drizzle glaze over the cookies while they're still warm. Sprinkle walnut chips over the wet glaze.

equipment

- measuring cups and spoons
- mixing bowl
- electric mixer
- spoon
- greased cookie sheet
- oven mitts
- metal spatula
- wire cooling rack

Yield: 4 dozen cookies

ingredients

- 2 sticks (1 cup) butter, softened
- 1½ cups (packed) brown sugar
- 2 eggs
- 2 teaspoons vanilla extract
- 1½ cups all-purpose flour
- 1½ cups cocoa powder
- 1 teaspoon baking soda
- ½ teaspoon salt
- 1½ cups chocolate chips

Day of the *Ninja*
December 5

Stealthy Chocolate Cookies

The ancient order of the Dark Chocolate Ninja Warriors is an enigma wrapped in a secret. Or maybe swallowed by a secret—these cookies have a mysterious way of disappearing.

1 Preheat the oven to 375°F. Cream the butter and brown sugar. Add the eggs and vanilla extract. Beat until combined.

2 Add the flour, cocoa powder, baking soda, and salt to the wet mixture. Mix well.

3 Add the chocolate chips. Scrape the bottom of the bowl to make sure everything is evenly blended.

4 Drop spoonfuls of dough a couple of inches apart on the cookie sheet. Bake 8 to 10 minutes. Use oven mitts to remove the cookies from the oven.

5 Use the metal spatula to transfer the cookies to the cooling rack. Remember—the cookies have a tendency to disappear. Don't let them out of your sight until you are ready to take a bite!

Walnut Rugelach

Spin the dreidel, light the menorah, and stuff your mouth with rolled-up, cinnamon-spiced cookies.

Yield: 2 dozen cookies

ingredients

- 2 sticks (1 cup) butter, softened
- 8-ounce package of cream cheese, softened
- 2 cups flour
- ½ cup (packed) brown sugar
- ½ cup walnuts
- ½ teaspoon ground cinnamon
- ½ teaspoon vanilla extract
- egg wash (page 14)
- sugar

equipment

- measuring cups and spoons
- mixing bowl
- electric mixer
- plastic wrap
- food processor
- lightly floured pastry board
- rolling pin
- paring knife
- greased cookie sheet
- pastry brush
- oven mitts
- metal spatula
- wire cooling rack

1 Cream the butter and cream cheese. Add the flour. Mix until the dough comes together in a ball. Divide the dough in half. Wrap each half in plastic wrap, and mash them into discs about ½ inch thick. Chill the cookie dough for at least 30 minutes.

2 While the dough is chilling, put the brown sugar, walnuts, cinnamon, and vanilla extract in the food processor. Process until the mixture is sandy.

3 Preheat the oven to 350°F. Sprinkle flour on the rolling pin. Working with one disc of chilled dough at a time, roll the dough out into a circle ⅛ to ¼ inch thick. Cut the circle into 12 wedges, as if you were cutting a pizza.

4 Spread half of the nut mixture over the "pizza." Roll each wedge up, starting from the wide end. (See photo.) Place the rugelach 1 inch apart on the greased cookie sheet. Brush some egg wash on top of each cookie. Sprinkle the cookies with sugar.

5 Repeat steps 3 and 4 with the other half of the dough. Bake these cookies for 28 to 30 minutes. Use oven mitts to remove the cookies from the oven. Let the baked rugelach cool on the pan for a couple of minutes. Then use the spatula to transfer them to the cooling rack.

equipment

- measuring cups and spoons
- 2 mixing bowls
- electric mixer
- plastic wrap
- lightly floured pastry board
- rolling pin
- snowflake-shaped cookie cutters
- greased cookie sheet
- whisk
- metal spatula
- wire cooling rack
- waxed paper
- spoon

ingredients

- 2 sticks (1 cup) butter, softened
- 1½ cups sugar
- 2 eggs
- 1 tablespoon vanilla extract
- 3 cups flour
- ½ teaspoon salt
- 1 pound (4 cups) powdered sugar
- ½ cup milk
- sparkly decorators' sugar

Winter Solstice

December 21 or 22 (Northern Hemisphere)

Sparkle Snowflakes

It's the shortest day and longest night of the year. Cozy up with a good book, a hot drink, and these beautiful cookies.

Yield: 3 to 4 dozen snowflakes, depending on the size of your cookie cutters

1 Cream the butter and sugar. Add the eggs and vanilla extract. Beat until well blended.

2 Add the flour and salt. Blend well. Divide the dough in half. Wrap each half in plastic wrap. Mash them into discs about ½ inch thick. Chill for at least 15 minutes.

3 Preheat the oven to 375°F. Sprinkle flour on the rolling pin. Roll each disc of dough out to about ¼ inch thick. Use the cookie cutter to cut out snowflake shapes. Squish the dough scraps together. Repeat the wrapping, mashing, chilling, rolling, and cutting.

4 Place the snowflakes 1 inch apart on the greased cookie sheet. Bake these cookies for 8 to 10 minutes. While the cookies bake, whisk the milk and powdered sugar together to make a glaze.

5 Use oven mitts to remove the cookies from the oven. Let the cookies cool a bit. Then use the spatula to transfer the still-warm cookies to the cooling rack. Put a sheet of waxed paper under the rack. Spoon glaze over the warm cookies. Sprinkle sparkle sugar on the wet glaze. (The waxed paper will catch the dripping glaze and spilled sugar.)

Sugar & Spice

Mexican and American influences combine in this recipe. The pretty cookies are also known as bizcochitos.

equipment

- measuring cups and spoons
- mixing bowl
- electric mixer
- plastic wrap
- bowl
- pastry board
- rolling pin
- cookie cutter— the fleur-de-lis shape is traditional
- greased cookie sheet
- oven mitts
- metal spatula
- wire cooling rack

Yield: about 3 dozen cookies

ingredients

- 2 sticks (1 cup) butter, softened
- 2/3 cup sugar
- 2 eggs
- 3 cups flour
- 1 teaspoon baking powder
- 1/2 teaspoon salt
- 1 to 3 teaspoons ground anise (Smell yours to see how strong it is. If it's weak, use the greater amount.)
- 1/2 cup sugar
- 2 tablespoons ground cinnamon

1 Cream the butter and 2/3 cup of sugar. Add the eggs. Beat until well blended.

2 Add the flour, baking powder, salt, and anise to the butter mixture. Blend well. Divide the dough in half. Wrap each half in plastic wrap, and mash them into discs about 1/2 inch thick. Chill the cookie dough for at least 20 minutes.

3 Preheat the oven to 350°F. Stir the 1/2 cup of sugar together with the cinnamon. Sprinkle one quarter of the cinnamon-sugar on the pastry board. Put one disc of chilled dough on the board, and then sprinkle another quarter of the cinnamon-sugar on top. Roll the dough out to about 1/4 inch thick, turning it often to make sure it's evenly coated with cinnamon-sugar. Use the cookie cutter to cut out cookies. Repeat this step with the other disc of chilled dough, using the remaining cinnamon-sugar.

4 Place the cookies 1 inch apart on the greased cookie sheet. Bake these cookies for 8 to 10 minutes. Use oven mitts to remove the cookies from the oven. Let the baked cookies cool on the pan for a couple of minutes. Then use the spatula to transfer the cookies to the cooling rack.

Tip: Squish your dough scraps together, and chill them again. When you roll them out this time, just use plain flour on your board. These cookies won't look the same as the official bizcochitos, but they sure are tasty!

equipment

- measuring cups and spoons
- 2 mixing bowls
- electric mixer
- whisk
- pastry board
- rolling pin
- person-shaped cookie cutter
- greased cookie sheet
- oven mitts
- metal spatula
- wire cooling rack
- pastry bag (page 15)

ingredients

- ½ stick (¼ cup) butter, softened
- ½ cup (packed) brown sugar
- ½ cup molasses
- 1 teaspoon vanilla extract
- 3½ cups flour
- 1 teaspoon baking soda
- ¼ teaspoon salt
- 1 tablespoon ground ginger
- ½ teaspoon ground cinnamon
- ¼ teaspoon ground cloves
- ¼ cup water
- Royal Icing (page 15)
- candies and fruit leather

Christmas
December 25

Gingerbread People

Make a batch of these sweet and spicy folks to rock around your Christmas tree.

Yield: totally depends on the size of your cookie cutter

1 Preheat the oven to 375°F. Cream the butter and brown sugar. Add the molasses and vanilla extract. Beat until well blended.

2 In another bowl, combine the flour, baking soda, salt, and spices. Whisk until the whole mixture is the same color.

3 Add the dry ingredients to the butter mixture. Use the lowest speed on the mixer to mix the dough. Add the water, and mix the dough until it's well blended.

4 This dough isn't very sticky, so you don't need to flour your pastry board or rolling pin. (Besides, you don't want white streaks on your finished cookies.) Roll out the dough to about ¼ inch thick.

5 Use the cookie cutter to cut out your gingerbread people. Place the cookies about 1 inch apart on the greased cookie sheet. Bake 8 to 10 minutes. (Giant cookies might take 12 minutes.)

6 Use oven mitts to remove the cookies from the oven. Let the cookies rest on the pan for a couple of minutes. Use the metal spatula to move the cookies to the cooling rack.

7 Use Royal Icing to glue outfits onto the cookies. Don't forget to leave cookies for Santa!

Benne Wafers

Whether you say sesame or benne, these little African seeds create a great crunch in a delicious little cookie!

Yield: about 3 dozen wafers

ingredients

- 1/2 cup sesame (benne) seeds
- 1/2 stick (1/4 cup) butter
- 2 tablespoons sesame oil
- 3/4 cup (packed) brown sugar
- 1/2 cup flour
- 1 egg
- 3/4 teaspoon vanilla extract
- 1/8 teaspoon baking powder
- 1/8 teaspoon salt

1 Preheat the oven to 375°F. Toast the sesame seeds in the frying pan over medium heat, stirring occasionally. If your pan isn't too heavy, this is a good chance to practice that fancy flip thing that professional chefs do. Scoot the pan toward the back of the burner, tilting it so the seeds pile toward the back of the pan. Now do a quick flick of your wrist, forward and up. Not a big flip, or the seeds might fly out of the pan! A few little flips will ensure that all the seeds get toasted evenly. Or use the spatula. When you smell a toasty, roasty scent, the sesame seeds are done.

2 Turn the stove off, and dump the sesame seeds into the mixing bowl. Put the butter in the pan. Let the residual heat melt it. Add the melted butter to the sesame seeds.

3 Add the sesame oil, brown sugar, flour, egg, vanilla extract, baking powder, and salt to the mixing bowl. Stir the ingredients until the mixture is smooth and gloppy, like caramel sauce.

4 Drop about 2 teaspoons of batter onto the parchment-lined cookie sheet. These wafers spread a lot, so leave 3 inches between each cookie.

5 Bake the benne wafers 4 to 6 minutes, until the edges are browned. (If you have a window in your oven door, turn on the oven light and watch the cookies bake. They go through a really cool transformation.) Use oven mitts to remove the cookies from the oven. Let the cookies cool on the pan for a few minutes. Then, peel them off the parchment paper and put them on a wire rack to finish cooling.

equipment

- measuring cups and spoons
- 2 mixing bowls
- electric mixer
- plastic wrap
- food processor
- whisk
- knife
- lightly floured pastry board
- rolling pin
- medium-sized round cookie cutter
- small round cookie cutter
- greased cookie sheet
- pastry brush
- oven mitts
- metal spatula
- wire cooling rack

ingredients

- 2 sticks (1 cup) butter, softened
- 1/4 cup heavy cream
- 2 cups sugar, divided
- 3 cups flour
- 2 cups sliced almonds
- 2 egg whites
- juice of half a lemon

New Year's Eve
December 31

Rahm-Ringel

Ringel in the new year with these fancy German ring-shaped cookies. (I saved the best for last.)

Yield: about 4 dozen ringels

1 Cream the butter, cream, and 1 cup of sugar. Turn the mixer down to medium, and add the flour one cup at a time. Mix until the dough pulls away from the bowl's sides.

2 Divide the dough in half. Wrap each half in plastic wrap. Mash the dough into flat discs. Chill the dough discs in the fridge for 1 hour. Meanwhile, coarsely grind the almonds in the food processor. Set the almonds aside. Whisk the egg whites together with the remaining 1 cup of sugar and the lemon juice.

3 Preheat the oven to 350°F. Flour the rolling pin. Unwrap and roll one dough disc to 1/4 thick. Cut rings of dough with the medium-sized cookie cutter. Then cut out each center with the small cutter. Place the dough rings on the greased cookie sheet. Repeat this step with the second disc of dough. Then make another disc from the scraps. Chill it, roll it out, and cut more rings.

4 Whisk the egg-white mixture to re-blend the sugar that has settled to the bottom of the bowl. Paint this mixture onto the cookies with the pastry brush. Sprinkle the ground almonds on top of the cookies.

5 Bake the cookies for 13 to 15 minutes, until the edges of the cookies are slightly browned. Use the oven mitts to remove the cookies from the oven. Let them cool for 10 minutes before transferring them to the wire rack.

Equipment Glossary

Serrated knife

Chef's knife

Paring knife

Scoop (solid) measuring cups

Wooden spoons

Liquid measuring cup

Sifter

Metal spatula

Measuring spoons

Rubber spatulas

Microplane grater

Box grater

Whisk

Cookie press with discs

Cutting/pastry boards

Electric mixer
with beaters

Mixing bowls

Sauce pots

Cooling rack

Cookie cutters

Cookie/baking sheet

Food processor

Baking dish

Glossary

Bake: cook in an oven. When the oven is set on "bake" the heat comes from the bottom of the oven and cooks food evenly from all sides.

Baking rack: the wire shelf in the oven.

Batch: the amount of cookies baked together at one time. If you have only one cookie sheet, you can bake a recipe in two or three batches.

Batter: liquid dough.

Beat: stir quickly with a fork, electric mixer, or whisk until well combined and a bit fluffy.

Beaters: the attachments on an electric mixer. Dip them into the bowl of ingredients to cream, beat, or whip.

Chill: to put dough in the refrigerator to cool so it's easier to work with.

Cooling rack: a wire rack to place cookies on to cool.

Cream: to mix softened butter and sugar.

Cutout cookie: a cookie that you cut from dough in a shape.

Divide: to separate into more than one part.

Drop cookie: a cookie formed by dropping a spoonful of dough onto a cookie sheet.

Equipment: another word for tools.

Extract: a flavored, edible liquid compound. Common extracts include vanilla and peppermint. A little extract goes a long way.

F: the abbreviation for Fahrenheit, which is a scale of measuring temperature.

Fold: to gently incorporate an ingredient into fluffy batter using a rubber spatula.

Fondant: a fairly thin, sugary mixture for decorating desserts.

Flouring: sprinkling flour on your pastry board and rolling pin so dough doesn't stick to them.

Frosting: a soft, thick, rich icing for desserts.

Glaze: a thin, sweet icing for desserts.

Grate: to use a grater to cut small pieces of food.

Grease: rubbing butter or oil on a baking pan so the food won't stick to it.

Greased: what a pan is after you grease it.

Icing: a sugary, decorative (and often delicious) coating for desserts.

Ingredients: all the different foods that go into a recipe.

Knead: mash dough with the heels of your hands.

Measuring spoons: tools for getting small amounts of an ingredient.

Offset spatula: a spreading tool with a bent blade.

Oven mitt: a tool that keeps you from burning your hands when you handle hot cookie sheets.

Pack: to squish an ingredient down into the measuring cup as you fill it.

Parchment paper: a non-stick paper for baking.

Pastry board: a handy wooden or plastic board that's good for rolling, shaping, and cutting dough. A cutting board can double as a pastry board.

Preheat: letting the oven heat up to the right temperature before you bake in it. Some ovens have a preheat setting, but you just turn most to "bake."

Purée: to blend into a smooth liquid or goo.

Recipe: a plan for making food.

Rest: what you do after you clean up the kitchen. Seriously, though, sometimes dough needs to relax after all that mixing.

Rolling pin: a tool for flattening dough. It has handles on each end that stay steady as the roller rotates.

Soften: to let an ingredient warm up to room temperature so it's squishy and easy to work with.

Sprinkles: tiny candy topping.

Substitute: use a different ingredient.

Utensil: a small tool with a handle.

Waxed paper: a non-stick paper used in preparing foods.

Whip: to mix food very fast to make a food such as icing super-fluffy.

Whisk: the name of a tool, and the action of using it.

Yield: how many servings a recipe makes.

Zest: the colored part of the peel of citrus fruits.

Metrics

Need to convert the measurements in this book to metrics? Here's how:
To convert degrees Fahrenheit to degrees Celsius, subtract 32 and then multiply by .56.
To convert inches to centimeters, multiply by 2.5.
To convert ounces to grams, multiply by 28.
To convert teaspoons to milliliters, multiply by 5.
To convert tablespoons to milliliters, multiply by 15.
To convert cups to liters, multiply by .24.

Index

Like this book? Check out my other cookbooks.

Bake It Up! Desserts, Breads, Entire Meals & More
Find dozens of doable recipes for breakfasts, lunches, dinners, and desserts. Try biscuits, sticky rolls, and a strata casserole, plus chicken fingers, tamale pie, and stromboli. Your family will ask you to be the house chef!

Delicious Drinks to Sip, Slurp, Gulp & Guzzle
It's full of easy recipes for smoothies, slushies, shakes, hot drinks, and more. Some of these drinks double as light, healthy meals. There are dairy-free options, too. Find recipes for every occasion and every taste.

Big Snacks, Little Meals After School, Dinnertime, Anytime
Satisfy your cravings! Chapters are divided by how you eat: with your fingers, by the handful, with a fork, with a spoon. Many of these recipes are perfect for sharing.

Super Sandwiches Wrap 'em, Stack 'em, Stuff 'em
Find classic sandwiches, trendy sandwiches, and sandwiches you've never heard of—because I made them up! Forget PB&J—try something hot, cold, spicy, sweet, toasted, grilled, or baked. The book includes easy ideas for breakfasts, lunches, dinners, and snacking.

Sweet Eats Mmmore Than Just Desserts
Delicious desserts and snacks don't need to come in a wrapper. Easily make whatever you want whenever you want it. Cobblers, pies, sundaes, cakes, fudge, nut bars—you get the idea!

The Greatest Cookies Ever Dozens of Delicious, Chewy, Chunky, Fun & Foolproof Recipes Many of these 75 recipes are like art projects, for ultimate play-with-your-food fun. Make classic chocolate chip or sugar cookies, or one-of-a-kind bugs or sea creatures. Yummy recipes with less sugar and fat are included.